GOD'S ANSWER TO FEAR WORRY ANXIETY

GREG LAURIE

GOD'S ANSWER TO FEAR, WORRY, AND ANXIETY
By GREG LAURIE

Copyright © 2019 Greg Laurie. All rights reserved.

Published by Harvest Ministries

www.harvest.org

ISBN-13 9781617540141

1 2 3 4 5 6 7 8 / 21 20 19

CONTENTS

WORRY | 31

ANXIETY | 61

GOD'S ANSWER FOR FEAR, WORRY, ANXIETY | 83

INTRODUCTION

Three o'clock in the morning and your mind is racing with all kinds of terrible thoughts taunting you, like proverbial monsters in the night. Maybe they woke you from a dead sleep, and they plague your mind like the ghosts of a nightmare you can't shake. Or perhaps you've been awake all night, your anxious thoughts keeping you from rest with their constant prodding, poking, and mocking.

What is it about those darkest hours of the night that make all of your fears, worries, and anxieties so much more intense? They're like Gremlins. If you feed them past midnight, they just get uglier and more destructive.

Many of us as children were afraid of the dark. Darkness is a representation of the unknown. As we grow older, we learn to not be afraid of the dark, but there's something about those midnight hours of sleeplessness that hearkens back to those childhood fears. We may not actually be scared of the physical darkness, but the unknown still grips us with anxiety.

God has an answer to your fear, worry, and anxiety.

What if this happens?
What if that happens?
What if the worst happens?

When a child is afraid of the dark, the best possible comfort to them, beyond turning on the lights, is the presence of a strong, confident adult that they know and trust and love—usually a mother or father.

The same is true for you and me in those wee hours of the morning when anxious notions come sweeping into our mind, uninvited and unwelcome. The presence of our heavenly Father has the power to set things right and bring us the peace we long for.

I want to tell you more about how God can dispel the shadows of fear, break the chains of worry, and slay the giant Anxiety. There is freedom in Christ!

God has an answer to your fear, worry, and anxiety if you will only cling to Him like a child in the darkness.

GOD'S ANSWER TO FEAR WORRY ANXIETY

FEAR

WORRY

ANXIETY

We all know the terrible sensation of fear. Oddly enough, many of us pay money to experience the emotion. We go to a scary movie and wait for the big, suspense-filled scene. The music builds, we know that something horrible is going to happen, and just as the big moment arrives . . . we put our hands over our ears and cover our eyes!

Others like to experience the thrill firsthand on some extreme ride at an amusement park. Back in the '60s, I used to ride a roller coaster that has since been torn down. It was really terrifying, especially since it had an ominous reputation. We all knew that cars had actually flown off the track before, so it was all the more thrilling to think, "I may not survive this!" The artificial feeling of danger was exciting.

Sometimes, though, we are afraid because our lives truly are in danger. Many of us have frightening memories of coming close to death, and all of us can remember a time when we thought our lives were almost over.

I once heard a story of a hitchhiker. A man in a pickup truck stopped for him. He hopped in the back and saw there was an empty coffin. It started to rain. The man was getting drenched, so he decided to use the coffin to escape from the storm. He opened it, climbed in, and pulled the lid shut. Inside, he was warm, and the hum of the truck engine put him to sleep.

We all know the terrible sensation of fear.

The truck driver saw two more hitchhikers and stopped to pick them up as well. They jumped in the back and were leaning on the coffin as the truck rolled along. Suddenly the first hitchhiker woke up, opened the lid and said, "Well, it must've stopped raining!" The other two men jumped out of the truck without waiting to ask questions. Now that's fear!

Those moments of physical fear that grip us in times of danger and help to keep us safe are not really what I'm concerned about in this book. Self-preservation and natural reflexes to flee from true and present dangers can be a good thing. God gave us adrenaline for a reason!

What I'm more concerned with is the fear that gnaws at us over time. It's the fear of the unknown, the fear of losing something we have, the fear of missing out on what's best, the fear of losing control, the fear of the future.

WHEN FEAR IS IN THE AIR

There's a lot of scary stuff out there. So many stresses and pressures that we have to contend with. There are legitimate threats and dangers in our world today. Fear is in the air all around us.

There is uncertainty in our country and around the world. Political strain, threats from terrorism, uncertainty about the future and about those who are in positions of leadership—and all of the garbage that the news media puts in front of our eyes each day.

Not only are there global fears; there are personal fears as well. We are afraid of losing our health. We are afraid of losing a member of our family. We are afraid of not having enough money. There is so much fear about so many things.

FEARS AND PHOBIAS

Some people have even taken fear to the next level, suffering from actual phobias that have a crippling effect on their lives. I read that the National Institute of Mental Health reports a significant increase in the number of Americans whose fears have moved into full-blown anxiety, disorders, and phobias.

To some degree, we all understand certain fears, like a fear of heights, or small spaces, or flying, or public speaking, or even dentists. But now there are all of these other phobias, and some are quite weird. I was reading through a list recently, and I couldn't believe some of these things were actual phobias.

There is one called cathisophobia which is the fear of sitting down. Wow, really? Then there is ablutophobia, the fear of bathing. Automatonophobia is the fear of wax figures, humanoid robots, ventriloquist's dummies. Alektorophobia: the fear of chickens. (Scary!) Peladophobia is the fear of baldness and bald people. If you have that fear, you don't want to meet me in person! And of course, phobophobia is the fear of phobias—because, why not?

Some of these are quite laughable, but in all seriousness, fear is no laughing matter. It is an emotion we are all quite familiar with. You know what it is like to be gripped by it. That shiver down the spine, the hairs standing on the back of your neck, your stomach sinking, and then your mouth goes dry. We have all experienced that in life at different times.

Jesus says, "Do not fear, little flock, for it is your Father's good pleasure to give you the kingdom" (Luke 12:32). In this short statement of Jesus, we see that we are sheep and Jesus is our Shepherd. Jesus is saying, "I am the Shepherd. I am going to watch out for you. I am going to protect you. Though you are defenseless, though you are weak, I am going to watch out for you. So don't be afraid, little flock."

If you are a child of God, you don't have to fear.

What comforting words Jesus speaks to us. If you are a child of God, you don't have to fear. Jesus is going to watch over you. But how do we put that head knowledge into our hearts and really apply it to our lives?

FEARFUL DISCIPLES

John 14 tells us of a time when the disciples were afraid. Jesus had dropped a bombshell on them. He said something that turned their world, as they knew it, upside down. He revealed that He would be betrayed, that He was going away, and that they could not come with Him.

But then He went on to share some words to bring calm in place of fear: "Don't let your hearts be troubled. Trust in God, and trust also in me" (John 14:1 NLT). He didn't say, "Mull over your problems." Rather, He said, "Don't be troubled."

Life is filled with trouble. It seems as though once you have one problem resolved, three more take its place. As Job 5:7 says, "People are born for trouble as readily as sparks fly up from a fire" (NLT). From the moment we come into this life, there are all kinds of troubles.

While there are reasons to be troubled, there is a greater reason not to be: We know Jesus.

While there are reasons to be troubled, there is a greater reason not to be: We know Jesus. He said to His disciples, "Trust in God, and trust also in me" (John 14:1 NLT). In other words, "I haven't brought you this far to abandon you now. I know what I'm doing. Believe."

There are times in our lives when things happen that we just don't understand. When I don't understand something about God, I try to always fall back on what I do understand: I do understand that God loves me. I do understand that He is looking out for me with my best interests in mind. And I do understand that no matter what happens, He will get me through.

The Bible contains a particularly interesting story about another time when Jesus' disciples were afraid:

> When evening had come, [Jesus] said to [His disciples], "Let us cross over to the other side." Now when they had left the multitude, they took Him along in the boat as He was. And other little boats were also with Him. And a great windstorm arose, and the waves beat into the boat, so that it was already filling. But He was in the stern, asleep on a pillow. And they awoke Him and said to Him, "Teacher, do You not care that we are perishing?"
>
> Then He arose and rebuked the wind, and said to the sea, "Peace, be still!" And the wind ceased and there was a great calm. But He said to them, "Why are you so fearful? How is it that you have no faith?"
>
> And they feared exceedingly, and said to one another, "Who can this be, that even the wind and the sea obey Him!"
>
> *Mark 4:35–41*

This particular day had been a long, exhausting one for Jesus. Though He was God, He allowed Himself to feel the frailties and the weaknesses of humanity. He did not sin, but He experienced the limitations of the human body. He had poured Himself out to His disciples and others, teaching them a series of very important parables, and He was dog-tired. So after He finished speaking, they loaded their weary Master into the boat. They took no supplies; they made no preparation. They just cast off from the shore and went.

But Jesus knew that school for His boys that day was not yet out of session. He wasn't finished teaching His disciples. A storm was brewing, and it was soon going to be time to put the day's lessons into action. All through the day, Jesus had been preparing His disciples for the storm. Now the time had come for a practical test. The storm was just a part of the day's curriculum. Had they been listening? The test would reveal the answer.

God gives many of us tests by surprise, and quite often they hit like a storm. He seldom tells us when a test is coming. He doesn't say, "Now brace yourself! I'm going to test you on this information. You'd better be paying attention!" God's tests usually come without warning. He wants our reactions to be pure, so that we can truly see the strength of our convictions.

We don't know when something fearful will suddenly drop into our lives. We don't know when tragedy will hit. We don't necessarily know when a crisis is coming or when we are going to face hardships. But God does! He knows when we are ready for them. If it were up to us, we would most likely always say, "I'm not ready yet, Lord."

The Bible tells us, "Count it all joy when you fall into various trials, knowing that the testing of your faith produces patience. But let patience have its perfect work, that you may be perfect and complete, lacking nothing" (James 1:2–4).

God not only tests, but He also re-tests us on the same material! Sometimes I think, "I've got that now! I know how to trust God in that area. I know how to look to God when the chips are down. I know how to deal with this situation. Please, no more tests on that subject."

But James gives good advice. Sometimes, it helps to see these trials as evidence of God's work in our lives. Remembering that He is still molding us and working to make us complete can help sustain us.

FEARFUL TRIALS WILL COME

In the Sermon on the Mount, Jesus gave an incredible series of teachings on how to live as His disciples. At the end of that teaching He said,

"Therefore whoever hears these sayings of Mine, and does them, I will liken him to a wise man who built his house on the rock: and the rain descended, the floods came, and the winds blew and beat on that house; and it did not fall, for it was founded on the rock.

But everyone who hears these sayings of Mine, and does not do them, will be like a foolish man who built his house on the sand: and the rain descended, the floods came, and the winds blew and beat on that house; and it fell. And great was its fall."

Matthew 7:24–27

Notice Jesus said that the rain did come. He didn't mention any exclusions or exceptions. There was no qualifier, such as "*If* the rain comes . . . ." Storms *will* come into every life. Every one of us will face times of testing, times of trial, and times of hardship. We will all encounter episodes of fear, worry, and anxiety. It is a part of life. No one is exempt. Remember, James said the same thing: *when* you fall into trials, not *if* (see James 1:2).

Believers can find comfort in the promises of God.

Quite simply, everyone is going to face hardships—the Christian and the non-Christian. But believers can find comfort in the promises of God. The nonbeliever has nothing to fall back on.

If you are building your life on the crumbling sand of family and friends alone, it will come as a shock when they abandon you just when you need them most.

If you're building your life on possessions, you'll find that they have no meaning when you're standing at death's door. The model of your car, the size of your bank account and your home become meaningless when you learn that you have a terminal illness.

> Everything, except the hope you have in Christ, will leave you empty.

Even religion, when it is mere ritual, can disappoint you. Everything, except the hope you have in Christ, will leave you empty.

The real question about life's storms is whether they will build you up or tear you down, strengthen you or destroy you, make you better or make you bitter.

FAITH, NOT FEAR

The apostle Paul gave us a promise worth remembering: "We know that all things work together for good to those who love God, to those who are the called according to His purpose" (Romans 8:28). This is a great verse for people who are going through hard times. Believers in Christ have hope and comfort, even if the enemy, Satan, attacks. Why? Because God is directing the proceedings. Even Satan's attempts must go through the screening process of God's love (see Job 1–2). If God allows you to be tested or to be tempted by the devil, rest assured that He has also put His protection around your life. As Warren Wiersbe said, "When God puts His own people into the furnace, He keeps His eye on the clock and His hand on the thermostat." So hold on to your faith.

The apostle Paul encouraged us in our hard times when he wrote, "Now no chastening seems to be joyful for the present, but painful; nevertheless, afterward it yields the peaceable fruit of righteousness to those who have been trained by it" (Hebrews 12:11). Let's be truthful: no one enjoys crisis. No one revels in difficulty. No one takes pleasure in going through hardship. But hardships do come and they are followed by real spiritual growth and fruit in our lives. Those are blessings that are worth holding on for.

Picture a young man in great physical condition. His biceps are bulging. His abs are like a washboard. We may think, "I want to look like that! That's great! I'm going to get in shape!" Motivated by this newfound goal, we rush off to the nearest gym to start sculpting our new dream physique. We work out for a while, then our muscles begin to throb and ache. The next day, it hurts to get out of bed. It even hurts to brush our teeth! We've called on muscles that have lain dormant for years, and every one of them is protesting! No matter how you approach that goal of becoming like that young man, it's going to hurt. That's just how the goal is achieved.

Sometimes when we say we want to grow in our faith as Christians, we will go through times of spiritual testing or stretching. And that often hurts too. Remember, "No pain, no gain!" Our transformation may be tough at times, but it is through these periods that we will grow and become stronger.

FEAR IS UNNECESSARY

After Jesus and His disciples set off on the waters, a furious squall came up. Huge waves engulfed the boat and terrified the seasoned sailors. These were experienced fishermen; they had lived through the worst of conditions. So if they were afraid, we have to conclude that this was an unusually fierce storm.

They cried out in despair for their lives. They thought they were going to die. But their fear was actually not necessary.

When the disciples began this journey, Jesus made a significant statement. Now, in the midst of the storm, they had already forgotten it, as we often forget God's Word in fearful times. If you look back, you will see that Jesus said, "Let us cross over to the other side" (Mark 4:35).

He was saying that they were going across the Sea of Galilee. He didn't say that they were going to get halfway across, confront a storm that would sink them, and all die together! He told them that they would arrive. He didn't promise that it would be a pleasant journey or smooth sailing. He didn't say they would not be met by winds and waves. But He did say that they would get across. There was comfort for the disciples in Jesus' simple words. In the storm, they simply forgot.

> No matter how long we have known the Lord or how many Bible verses we have memorized, we are still susceptible to fear and worry.

No matter how long we have known the Lord or how many Bible verses we have memorized, we are still susceptible to fear and worry when a crisis hits our lives. Often, we are paralyzed by fear, and we, too, forget what God has said.

GOD'S PROMISES KEEP FEAR IN CHECK

Many Bible verses contain comforting promises. What comfort there is in the apostle Paul's words: "He who has begun a good work in you will complete it until the day of Jesus Christ" (Philippians 1:6). He started it, and He's going to finish it. We must not give up on what we know to be true. Even when times are hard, even when we don't understand, we have God's promises to lean on.

Jesus said, "I am the good shepherd; and I know My sheep, and am known by My own . . . . they shall never perish; neither shall anyone snatch them out of My hand" (John 10:14, 28). We have nothing to fear as long as we stay close to Him, His Word, and His people. The devil's threats are empty. Believers are safe in God's hands. Nothing can hinder the working out of His plans.

> Even when times are hard, even when we don't understand, we have God's promises to lean on.

If you choose to run from God or rebel against Him, the outcome could be different. You're taking unnecessary chances by doing so. Stay close to Him and you'll be all right. It's better to be in the center of the storm with Jesus than anywhere else without Him.

JESUS IS WITH US

The disciples did not need to be afraid: Jesus was right there in the boat with them. He had just spent the day performing miracles and preaching truths in their presence, but they still lost heart. They despaired for their lives. They still did not understand the full extent of His power.

Just as Jesus was with the disciples, He is with us, too. The writer of Hebrews reminds us of the Lord's promise: "I will never leave you nor forsake you" (Hebrews 13:5). In the original Greek translation, it reads more like this: "I will never, no never, no never leave you nor forsake you." He also told His disciples before He ascended to Heaven, "I am with you always, even to the end of the age" (Matthew 28:20). If you are a Christian, God is with you too, wherever you go.

> Jesus is not only the light at the end of the tunnel. He is with you in the tunnel.

Jesus is not only the light at the end of the tunnel. He is with you in the tunnel. You may be discouraged now, but the Lord will see you through. You may have questions, but Jesus will take you to "the other side." Hold on to this truth. As King David, who knew quite a bit about personal suffering, wrote, "Yea, though I walk through the valley of the shadow of death, I will fear no evil; for You are with me" (Psalm 23:4).

WHAT ARE YOU AFRAID OF?

You may be thinking, "Wait a second! How can you say that God won't allow boats to sink in the storms of life? I know people who have died, and they were Christians! What about them? Why didn't God protect them?"

I don't know why God spares some and takes others, but death is not really the issue. We must all die sometime, and when we die those who know God will enter into His presence.

For the believer, death is not the worst possible outcome of a situation. Although we may not be looking forward to death, Jesus told us not to fear it. That's why the apostle Paul quoted Isaiah in saying, "O death, where is your victory? O death, where is your sting?" (1 Corinthians 15:55 NLT). As Christians, we don't necessarily look forward to dying, but at the same time, we don't have to be afraid, for we will "cross over to the other side," safe in the arms of Jesus. The apostle Paul also told us, "For we know that if our earthly house, this tent, is destroyed, we have a building from God, a house not made with hands, eternal in the heavens" (2 Corinthians 5:1).

> Do you fear the future? God knows what lies ahead of you.

The disciples faced two possible outcomes during that storm. One would be for them to die and go immediately to Heaven. The alternative was that Jesus would deliver them and see them through. Whatever happened, they would be all right.

Do you fear the future? God knows what lies ahead of you. What if tragedy befalls you? God will see you through. What if you die? If Christ is your Savior and Lord, you will see Heaven and spend eternity in His glorious presence where there is fullness of joy and pleasures forevermore (see Psalm 16:11).

Again, the question should not be, "What if I die?" We must think in terms of "*When* I die . . ." We need to face the fact that we are going to die (unless Christ comes again first). We should not focus on what it will mean to cease to exist on this earth, but rather concentrate on the fact that when we die, we will go to Heaven and we will see God face to face. We are reminded in Scripture to "prepare to meet your God . . ." (Amos 4:12). Are you prepared? Remember, only those who are prepared to die are really ready to live.

Syndicated newspaper columnist Ann Landers received thousands of letters each month. When she was asked what problem was most dominant in the letters she received, Ann replied, "It's fear. People are afraid. They're afraid of losing their wealth. They're afraid of losing their health. They're afraid of losing loved ones. They're afraid of life itself!" We have no guarantee that our health will always be good. We have no guarantee that we won't lose our wealth. We have no guarantee that our loved ones will share all of this life with us.

God's servant Job lost everything in one day! He lost wealth, health, and loved ones. The Bible says, "In all this, Job did not sin by charging God with wrongdoing" (Job 1:22 NIV). But instead he said, "Naked I came from my mother's womb, and naked I will depart . . . . may the name of the LORD be praised" (Job 1:21 NIV). Because of Job's faithfulness during this trial, God replaced all that Satan was allowed to take from him. God restored his fortunes, in fact, God gave him twice as much as he had before.

This is not to suggest that loved ones can be replaced. But we can have comfort in knowing that we will see them again if they know Christ. That's a good reason to share the gospel with your family and friends. Death can be only a temporary separation through our love in Jesus Christ.

GOD HEARS OUR CRIES

What was Jesus doing during that storm on the sea? The storm was beating on the boat, waves towered overhead, and the boat was filling up with water while Jesus slept (see Mark 4:37–38).

He slept? How could He sleep through all that? He was in the same boat that the waves were crashing down on.

Apparently, the storm did not bother Jesus. But notice what *did* get His attention. It wasn't the wind. It wasn't the waves. It was the needs of His people. Just as a loving parent hears his child, so God always hears the cries of His children.

Notice how the disciples interpreted Jesus' actions. They said, "Teacher, do You not care that we are perishing?" (Mark 4:38). They may have been thinking, "What is the problem with You? You're lying there sleeping while we're drowning!"

They didn't say, "Jesus, do a miracle." They were afraid, and it bothered them that He was just lying there asleep, seemingly indifferent to their problems. Their attitude seemed to be,

God is never asleep when you call on Him.

"Lord, don't You care about what we're going through right now?"

They were wrong to be gripped by fear. They were wrong to speak to Jesus that way. They had lost sight of who He was. But they were right to call out to Jesus. As the apostle Paul said, "Whoever calls on the name of the Lord shall be saved" (Romans 10:13).

As a man, Jesus slept; but as God, He was in total control. God never sleeps! We don't have to wake God up. We don't have to yell and scream to get His attention. We only have to call upon His name. Psalm 121:4 teaches, "Behold, He who keeps Israel shall neither slumber nor sleep." God is never asleep when you call on Him. He's always ready to hear the cry of His children.

JESUS CARES

Sometimes, during the storms, we wonder if the sun will ever shine again. We feel that God does not care about our trials, that He doesn't see what's happening to us, that He doesn't realize the pain of our hardships, that He isn't interested in our lives.

That's how Martha felt about Jesus when He didn't arrive in Bethany in time to heal her brother, Lazarus, before he died. Jesus knew Lazarus was sick, but He intentionally took His time getting to him. As Lazarus got weaker, hours turned into days. Finally it was too late. Lazarus died. By the time Jesus arrived, Lazarus had been dead four days. Hope was gone. There

> Far too often, we call on the Lord as a last resort.

would be no healing. Jesus had let them down, or so they thought. But He had heard their cries, and He cared about them.

In her grief, Martha said, "Lord, if You had been here, my brother would not have died" (John 11:21). Martha and Mary had probably told everyone that they knew Jesus personally and that He would come when they called Him for help. They were depending on Jesus. After all, He was their friend. He had stayed at their house in Bethany on a number of occasions. He had dined with them. They were certain that Jesus, a true friend, would be there when they needed Him. But Jesus had not planned a healing; He had planned a resurrection! Jesus wanted to do more than they expected of Him.

Sometimes, we limit God with our prayers. We pray for one thing or another, and when God doesn't give it to us, we despair. But did you ever stop to think that God may want to go above and beyond all that we ask or think (see Ephesians 3:20)? That could be why He hasn't answered your prayer as you expected.

Sometimes, God comes quickly, and some-times, we must wait. God's delays are not necessarily denials. God does not necessarily work on our schedule. Sometimes, He is waiting for us to exhaust our resources and completely trust Him. Far too often, we call on the Lord as a last resort, when instead we should have known that He is our only hope.

While the disciples were afraid of the storm, Jesus remained calm. He simply got up in the boat, walked over to the side, and said, "Peace, be still." The words He used are actually better translated, "Be muzzled!" This must have seemed like an odd command. But to the disciples' surprise, the elements calmed down, the winds ceased, and the water turned to glass. They said, "Who can this be, that even the wind and the sea obey Him!" (Mark 4:41).

Jesus got right to the heart of the problem and silenced the storm with a word. When He was finished, the disciples faced something even more terrifying than the storm. They received the rebuke of Jesus. He turned to them and said, "Why are you so fearful? How is it that you have no faith?" (Mark 4:40). Those strong words shook the disciples. How much better it would have been to have weathered the storm and heard Him say, "Well done!"

FEAR AND UNCERTAINTY

How futile to worry about things that might never happen. What a waste to shift our focus from things that we know are certain and concern ourselves with things that might never come to pass! For instance, we worry about losing our health or wealth and forget to prepare ourselves for the judgment of God. We may or may not experience loss on earth, but we will surely stand before God one day.

Some people realize that after it's too late. There once lived a salty old sea captain who didn't believe in God's existence. One day, he was washed overboard by a wave. He thought he was drowning. As the waves rushed over him, he cried out to God for help. Sailors who heard his cry rescued him, but could not resist taunting him about calling on the God he didn't believe existed. "Well, if there is no God, there should be, in times like this!" he replied. He awoke to the truth almost too late!

How futile to worry about things that might never happen.

We should turn to God, and not only when the chips are down. Some people only cling to God in a crisis. They grasp for Him in the midst of a hardship or they turn to Him in the face of sickness or death. I want you to know that just as Jesus saved the disciples who cried, "Save us, Lord! We're perishing," God hears our cries. He is ready to receive us and forgive us regardless of what problems or circumstances bring us to our senses. He forgives the worry-filled thoughts we have. But He still wants us to trust Him, even with our lives.

I once received a letter from a man who came to one of our evangelistic outreaches. He told of a life filled with heartbreak. At the age of 29, he left his wife and two children for a homosexual lifestyle. His wife later remarried, but this man continued his chosen lifestyle until his partner died of AIDS.

No longer able to handle the loss of his companion and the fact that he now had AIDS too, the man tried to commit suicide. The doctors saw no reason why he should have survived his suicide attempt. But his children, who were Christians, were praying for him. And God had a different plan for their prodigal father.

When the man was released from the hospital, he began to long for a relationship with the living God. He attended that outreach event, heard the gospel, and made a commitment to Jesus Christ. He started reading the Bible and attending church. He was filled with joy, knowing that he would meet the Lord when he died. He wanted to spend his last days sharing God's love with others.

Thank God, we all can have hope, even when our situation appears utterly hopeless.

GOD'S PROTECTING PRESENCE

In Psalm 91, we find this promise for believers: "Though a thousand fall at your side, though ten thousand are dying around you, these evils will not touch you" (Psalm 91:7 NLT).

Isn't that great to know? It isn't over until it's over. Until that time, we can go out with boldness, knowing that God is in control of our lives. There is nothing to fear.

I read the story of a courageous Christian who was standing before a king who wanted him to deny Christ. The king threatened, "If you don't do it, I will banish you."

The Christian replied, "You can't banish me from Christ. He says He will never leave me nor forsake me."

The king said, "I will confiscate your property and take it all from you."

The Christian said, "My treasures are laid up on high; you cannot get them."

"I will kill you," the king told him.

"I have been dead forty years," the Christian answered. "I have been dead with Christ, dead to the world. My life is hidden with Christ in God, and you cannot touch it."

The king said, "What can you do with such a fanatic?"

May God make us people who know, rely on, and trust in His presence and protection like this believer did!

1 John 4:18 tells us that perfect love casts out fear, and 1 John 4:16 tells us that God is love. We do not need to fear when God is with us.

FEAR
WORRY
ANXIETY

Fear has a twin brother that he likes to hang out with. Fear's twin is Worry. Oftentimes Worry and Fear work in tandem. You can easily get caught up by these brothers and get dragged down spiritually.

In a recent Gallup poll, when people were asked about their previous day, 45% of Americans reported that they felt worried a lot, and 55% said they were stressed. These numbers are the highest they've ever been on record.[1]

There are two old sayings about worry that I really like. The first says: "Worry is the advance

---

[1] https://news.gallup.com/poll/249098/americans-stress-worry-anger-intensified-2018.aspx

interest you pay on troubles that seldom come." The second saying is "Worry is a lot like a rocking chair. It gives you something to do, but it never gets you anywhere."

The problem with worrying is that it never really helps a situation along. In fact, worrying often makes matters worse! Nine times out of ten, worry does more damage to the worrier than the problem does—even if "the worst" does happen! The worry often tears us up inside more than the events we dread.

Excessive worry, experts say, can actually shorten the human lifespan. Modern medical research has shown that worry actually breaks down our resistance to disease and wreaks havoc on the immune system. It can impact the nervous system, the digestive organs, and the heart. People can shave years off their lives because they are besieged by worry.

> The problem with worrying is that it never really helps a situation along.

I heard of one man who was a real worrywart. He had the reputation of being a compulsive worrier. One day, some of his friends saw him and noticed that he didn't seem to be worried at all. They remarked, "You're always worried about everything, but today you seem so calm and serene! What happened?"

"Well," he replied, "I hired someone to worry for me. I tell him all my problems, and he worries about them. I don't even have to think about them anymore." When his friends asked how he arranged for such a service, he answered, "I pay ten thousand dollars a month."

"How can you pay so much!" they said. "Where are you going to get ten thousand dollars a month?"

"That's for *him* to worry about," came the calm reply.

"NO WORRIES, MATE!"

When I was in Australia a number of years ago, I noticed they had an expression there that I really like. You will be talking to an Aussie and ask them a question, or ask them for directions. They are very friendly and they will usually respond: "No worries, mate!" And then they will answer your question or tell you how to get where you want to go.

I like that: "No worries, mate!" That is good theological advice. We have a lot of worries, don't we? A lot of things that weigh us down. A lot of things that concern us. We worry about what we are going to eat. We worry about what we are going to wear. We worry about where we are going to live. We worry about our employment. We worry about our family.

We worry when things are going well because we are concerned about when they are going to go bad. Then when they are bad, we worry about if they will ever be good again. We worry about everything.

Would you classify yourself as a worrier? I think of that great theologian Charlie Brown, who made this statement about worry: "I have developed a new philosophy. I only dread one day at a time." Are you a Charlie Brown when it comes to worry?

Now let me quote a real theologian, Dr. Martyn Lloyd-Jones, who said this: "If I allow my concern about the future to cripple me in the present, I am guilty of worry." The result of worrying about the future is that you cripple yourself in the present.

Studies have been done among Americans, asking them what they worry about the most. They are predictable things. Middle-age Americans worry most about their finances. They also worry about being audited by the IRS. (Maybe there is a connection there.) A growing concern today is a fear of being hacked—that someone would get your personal information, or that your smartphone or computer would be stolen.

> **The result of worrying about the future is that you cripple yourself in the present.**

There was an article that was out a while back about a bunch of celebrities who were upset because their phones had been hacked and now naked photos of these people are on the Internet. I have a thought about that: don't take pictures of yourself while you are naked—ever! That pretty much solves the problem, doesn't it?

Among the studies that have been done asking people what they worry about the most, usually at the top of the list is appearance. That is amazing. "I don't care if I lose my house or I die in a nuclear blast. How do I look in this outfit?" Also at the top of the list is usually the fear of public speaking. In fact, the fear of speaking in public is usually higher than the fear of dying! Can you imagine that? "You can die right now or give a short speech. What's it going to be?"

WORRY CAN GET US

There is an old fable that is told about the dangers of worry. As the story goes, Death was walking toward a city one morning. A man stopped Death and said, "Where are you going?" Death said, "I am going into that city to take a hundred people."

"That is horrible," the man says. Death responds, "That is what I do." The man ran ahead of Death to warn everyone he could. Evening fell and that man met Death again. The man said, "I thought you were only going to take a hundred people. Why did a thousand people die?"

Death responded, "I kept my word. I took only a hundred people. Worry took the rest."

That is how life can be. Worry can get us.

Did you know that 75–90 percent of all visits to primary care physicians are stress-related complaints or disorders? Know this: most of what we worry about never actually happens. Dr. Walter Calvert conducted a survey on worry that indicated only eight percent of the things people worried about were legitimate matters of concern and the other 92 percent were either imaginary or never happened.

> Know this: most of what we worry about never actually happens.

STOP WORRYING!

Christ Himself addresses the topic of worry in the Sermon on the Mount:

Therefore I say to you, do not worry about your life, what you will eat or what you will drink; nor about your body, what you will put on. Is not life more than food and the body more than clothing? Look at the birds of the air, for they neither sow nor reap nor gather into barns; yet your heavenly Father feeds them. Are you not of more value than they? Which of you by worrying can add one cubit to his stature?

So why do you worry about clothing? Consider the lilies of the field, how they grow: they neither toil nor spin; and yet I say to you that even Solomon in all his glory was not arrayed like one of these. Now if God so clothes the grass of the field, which today is, and tomorrow is thrown into the oven, will He not much more clothe you, O you of little faith?

Therefore do not worry, saying, "What shall we eat?" or "What shall we drink?" or "What shall we wear?" For after all these things the Gentiles seek. For your heavenly Father knows that you need all these things.

Matthew 6:25–32

Then comes the most important verse: "But seek first the kingdom of God and His righteousness, and all these things shall be added to you" (6:33). Every Christian should commit that verse in particular to memory.

Jesus is not saying that the believer should not be concerned about the necessities of life. He is not saying that we should not think about them or plan for the future. The Bible encourages us to work hard, to save our money, and so forth. What He is saying is that we should not *worry* about these things. Verse 25 plainly says: "Do not worry about your life." The word *worry* in the old English means to choke. Worry chokes you out.

One day I was playing with some of my grandkids. They started choking me. They thought that was very entertaining. Then they took it up a few notches and they were jumping on my back and grabbing me from behind. I said, "OK kids, let's back off a little bit. You are hurting Papa." They came back a few days later and asked, "Can we choke you again, Papa?" A great form of entertainment—choking your grandfather.

> The word *worry* in the old English means to choke. Worry chokes you out.

That is what worry does to us. It chokes us. It cuts us off. In the Greek, this command of Christ to not be anxious includes the idea of stopping what has already been done. Effectively, Jesus is saying, "Stop worrying about your life. Stop it. You have been doing it up to this point and you need to stop doing it."

WORRY IS NOT A VIRTUE

Interestingly, we tend to elevate worry as a virtue. "Because I care, I worry."

Wait a second. Is worry a virtue? I don't think it is at all. In fact, I think worry can be a sin. I am not saying all worry is a sin, but I am saying it can be a sin. And I would readily admit it is a sin I have committed. I have worried about things unnecessarily. I have fretted and been filled with anxiety just like you have.

Why is worry potentially a sin? Because it is a lack of trust in God. What I am really saying when I worry is, "God isn't in control. God is not taking care of me in this situation. I am not trusting in the providence of God." If you are a real Christian and you believe the Bible, you will know this: God is in control of all circumstances that surround your life and there are no accidents in the life of the Christian. That is an important thing to know.

> **What I am really saying when I worry is, "God isn't in control."**

Yet we will worry about a lot of things. Corrie ten Boom identifies the problem with worry: "Worry does not empty tomorrow of its sorrows. It empties today of its strength."

RESTING WITH THE LIONS

The story of Daniel is a good illustration of a guy who could have worried but didn't. His enemies hatched a plot to have him killed because they wanted him out of the way. They were jealous of his power and influence with the king. The king unwittingly signed into law a decree that no man could pray to any god but the king. Because Daniel was a man of prayer, he ended up in a den of lions—so he was going to die, no question about it.

The king spent the night worrying and Daniel spent the night sleeping like a baby.

By the way, I read an article in the paper about a man in a Ukrainian zoo. I guess he thought he was some kind of a modern Daniel. He decided to climb into the den of the lioness in the Kiev Zoo and he screamed out, "God will save me if He exists." Well, God exists, but He didn't save this crazy guy and the lion killed him immediately. There is a difference between trusting the Lord and testing the Lord.

Daniel was not testing the Lord. He was put into a lion's den because of his faithfulness to God. What is fascinating about this story is that the king himself could not reverse the law he ignorantly set into place, yet it was the king who spent the night worrying and Daniel spent the night sleeping like a baby. The guy in the lion's den had a good night's sleep. The guy in the palace did not.

That is how it is when you are walking right with God. You can just kick back and rest in Him. The Bible even says, "He gives His beloved sleep" (Psalm 127:2). I bet Daniel used one of those lions as a pillow. (I am sure a lion would be really comfortable to lie on, if it isn't hungry.)

THE SOLUTION FOR WORRY

The Bible tells us we should cast all of our care on Him, for He cares for us (see 1 Peter 5:7). It would be like if you just got off of a plane and you are carrying a bunch of extra weight. You have a lot of carry-on stuff. You have your backpack, you are schlepping along your roller bag, and you have another suitcase as well. A friend says, "Hey man, let me take that load." Your response is "Gladly! Thank you, buddy!" Jesus wants to take that load off of you. Take your worries and cast them on Christ.

I like what Martin Luther said: "Pray, and let God worry." Obviously, God is not going to worry. Prayer is the real secret. In Philippians, it says that you should not worry about anything but pray about everything, and the peace of God that passes all human understanding will keep your heart and mind in Christ Jesus (see Philippians 4:6–7). Turn your worries into prayers. The next time you are gripped by fear and worry—*What if this happens? What if that happens?*—turn it into a prayer. Send the worry straight to Heaven. "Lord, I don't know about this, but I trust You and You are in control and I commit this to You right now." We need to be looking to the Lord and allowing Him to give us His peace.

Turn your worries into prayers.

Jesus says, "Look at the birds. Do they worry?" Have you ever seen a stressed-out bird? Birds wake up every morning and they are just singing away. They are simply happy. No bird has ever been promised eternal life. No bird has ever been given the hope of Heaven. Yet they sing their hearts out every day. Jesus is not saying the birds sit by idly and wait for the food to come to them. They take action.

They go and get food for themselves. But they don't worry.

Then Jesus says, "Why do you worry about clothing? Consider the flowers of the field. They neither toil nor spin, and yet even Solomon the king in his royal robes was not dressed like one of these beautiful flowers" (see Matthew 6:28–29). So now He is talking about the way that you look—your appearance. We have a culture that is so obsessed with the way that they look. We are always wanting to look better—change our bodies. We want to look like those people on the magazine covers. The problem is, the people on the magazine covers don't even look like the people on the magazine covers! Have you ever heard of Photoshop? Those people you see on the covers don't exist in real life.

It is a good thing to want to look your best on the outside, but don't neglect the inside. You can have a chiseled body and a dying soul. The Bible even addresses that in 1 Peter 3. It says, "What matters is not your outer appearance—the styling of your hair, the jewelry you wear, the cut of your clothes—but your inner disposition. Cultivate inner beauty, the gentle, gracious kind that God delights in" (verses 3–4 MSG). This is so relevant for today. There is a place for staying in shape. I don't want you to misunderstand me and say, "It doesn't matter. I'll just let myself go. I want to be obese for God." No, that is going too far the other way.

WORRY DOESN'T MAKE YOUR LIFE LONGER

Here is what Jesus is saying: "Which of you by worrying can add one cubit to his stature?" (Matthew 6:27). Here would be a better translation for us: "Which of you by worrying could add one day to your life?" God determines the date of your birth and the date of your death. You have everything to say about that little dash in the middle and what you do with it. You cannot lengthen your life. Only God determines how long a man or a woman will live.

I watched a show on TV years ago about a guy who had made it past 100 years old. I waited until the end of this program to hear the guy's secret for living past 100. Want to know what he said? "Eat a hot dog every day." I'm telling the absolute truth. They took him into the supermarket and showed the hot dogs he bought, and they weren't Hebrew National. They were the cheap kind with rat tails in them—the ones that taste really good.

There is a balance we should keep in mind. As 1 Timothy 4:8 says, "Physical training is good, but training for godliness is much better, promising benefits in this life and in the life to come" (NLT).

No, worry doesn't make your life longer. It just makes it more miserable.

THE WORRY-FREE LIFE

Jesus gives us the secret to living a worry-free life. Instead of worry, put God and His will first in your life. Matthew 6:33 says, "Seek first the kingdom of God and His righteousness, and all these things shall be added to you." What does that mean?

The Greek translation of the word *first* means first in a line of more than one option. There are many options I can seek to live for in life. I can live for my phys-ical appearance. I can live for a successful career. I can live for having pleasures. I can live for a lot of things. But Jesus says that among all those options, put God in the number-one position. Seek first the kingdom of God. If you want a life free of worry, put God's kingdom before everything else.

> **Put God in the number-one position.**

You say, "Well, what does that mean?" Let's take your career for example. The business that you happen to be in. Ask yourself this question: "Is this career choice—this line of work that I am doing—really for God's glory?" In other words, "Am I seeking God first in what I am doing?"

You say, "Greg, you are a pastor. That is your job. It is easy for you to seek God first. My job is different than yours and I work in the real world with real people." I understand what you are saying, but here is what your goal should be: to honor God in everything that you do. I don't care what you do. If you can't honor God in what you do, get a new job.

> **Your goal should be: to honor God in everything that you do.**

Here is what you have to ask yourself: "As I am doing this thing, what is my goal?" If your goal is just to make money, no matter what it takes, you have got the wrong goal. Your goal should be to honor God, give honest work, and have personal integrity and a good testimony in the workplace.

I know Christians who are successful in business but have a bad reputation because they cut corners or don't do the job right. That's not good. When the day is done, you want to have a good name and a good reputation. Proverbs 22:1 says, "Choose a good reputation over great riches; being held in high esteem is better than silver or gold" (NLT).

There are people in life who do cut corners. There are people in life who cheat on the test and pass the exam when you studied hard. There are people in life who lie on their resumes and get the position you were hoping to get. There are people in life who flatter the boss and move up the ladder a little more quickly than you do. There are people in life who do it the wrong way, and get ahead in life. You say, "You see, the integrity thing doesn't work." Just hold on a minute, Buckaroo. If

When you seek God first, life will find its proper perspective.

you live a godly life and you live an honest life and have integrity and work hard, God is going to bless you for it. There will be times when others seem to be doing better than you, but just wait awhile and see how it plays out. The Bible says a person will reap what they sow.

It's a little bit like the tortoise and the hare. You are the tortoise, just doing your thing—walking with the Lord—doing it the right way. An honest day's work for an honest day's pay. Then, in time, you get that promotion or the other position. And just like that, you are elevated. I am not saying this will always happen. My point is simply this: God will honor it. You seek Him first and He will take care of you.

When you seek God first, life will find its proper perspective. "All these things shall be added to you." What things? The things Jesus talked about. What I'm going to eat. What I'm going to wear. We could expand that: Where I am going to live. Where I am going to work. What I am going to drive. What I am going to do. God is saying, "I will take care of those things if you will seek Me first."

The Lord came to Solomon, who was to replace his father as the King of Israel. Solomon's dad had died. The Lord came to this young man and said, "I will give you whatever you want. Ask it and I will give it." Can you imagine? What would you do if God came to you tonight and said, "I will give you whatever you want. You want riches? I will give you riches. You want fame? I will give you fame. What is it you want?"

Solomon says, "I want wisdom to rule your people." The Lord says, "That is good. I'll tell you what, buddy. I am going to give you the wisdom you asked for. And because you didn't ask for long life and riches, I am going to give you those things as well." Solomon demonstrated what it means to seek first the kingdom. He didn't seek that stuff. He sought God. And God said, "I am going to bless you for that."

IS THERE A LINK BETWEEN WORRY AND MONEY?

In Matthew 6:25, Jesus said: "Therefore I say to you, do not worry." Notice it starts with the word *therefore*.

Whenever you read the word *therefore* in the Bible, find out what it is *there for*. Jesus is drawing upon what has been previously said. What did Jesus say prior to this? We go back to Matthew 6:19–21: "Do not lay up for yourselves treasures on earth, where moth and rust destroy and where thieves break in and steal; but lay up for yourselves treasures in heaven, where neither moth nor rust destroys and where thieves do not break in and steal. For where your treasure is, there your heart will be also." Jesus is not saying it is wrong for you to have stuff. Effectively, He is saying it is wrong when stuff has you.

In fact, it is interesting that this phrase *lay up* is used. It means to lay something horizontally, as in storing it permanently. He is not talking about the man who is saving, but the man who is stockpiling. He is not talking to the woman who merely has possessions, but to the woman who has them to flaunt. Some people love to flaunt their stuff. They tell you what they paid for everything when you didn't even ask. "Do you know what I paid for this? Do you know how much that cost? I own this. I own that." Why? To impress people. Jesus says not to do that. Don't lay up treasures in that way. Seek first the kingdom.

> Many believers struggle financially today because they have not learned the simple principle of seeking first the kingdom in their giving.

Many believers struggle financially today because they have not learned the simple principle of seeking first the kingdom in their giving. The Bible tells us as Christians that we are to bring our tithes and our offerings to the Lord. By the way, those are two separate things. Every Christian should tithe. You say, "What is a tithe?" A tithe is ten percent. You bring your income to the Lord and give it to Him on a regular basis. An offering is above and beyond that. We say, "I can't afford to do that!" As far as I am concerned, I can't afford not to. I have found that when I am faithful in my giving to the Lord, He blesses me because I am seeking first His kingdom. That is exactly the context of this statement.

In fact, in Proverbs 3 we read of God saying, "Honor the LORD from your wealth and from the first of all your produce." That is seeking first the kingdom. "So your barns will be filled with plenty and your vats will overflow with new wine" (verses 9–10 NASB). God is saying, "You take care of this—you put Me first in all things—and I will take care of you."

Paul tells us that if you sow sparingly, you will reap sparingly. If you sow generously, you will reap generously (see 2 Corinthians 9:6). Put God first. Jesus says, "Give, and it will be given to you. A good measure, pressed down, shaken together and running over, will be poured into your lap. For with the measure you use, it will be measured to you" (Luke 6:38 NIV).

There is only one time in the Bible when God says, "Test Me on this. Put Me to the test on this." It is in the last book of the Old Testament, the Book of Malachi. God says, "Bring the whole tithe into the storehouse, that there may be food in my house. Test me in this . . . and see if I will not throw open the floodgates of heaven and pour out so much blessing that there will not be room enough to store it" (verse 3:10 NIV).

| Because we have received, we should give.

You say, "Greg, I think you are saying we should give to get." Not at all. If you think that, you are misunderstanding. Here is what I am saying: because we have received, we should give. The Bible says, "Freely you have received, freely give" (Matthew 10:8). This is not giving to obligate God. This is giving because God has done so much for us.

When I do this, I lay up for myself a treasure in Heaven. It's been said,

> "Do your giving
> While you're living.
> Then you're knowing
> Where it's going."

You can't take it with you, but you can send it on ahead.

WRESTLING VS. RESTING

Worry is kind of like wrestling, isn't it? It's a wearying struggle in your mind and heart. It reminds me of the story of Jacob wrestling with God.

Jacob was the kind of guy who didn't like to sit still. But in Genesis 32, he finds himself alone with God. And a wrestling match ensues. It is kind of humorous—Jacob wrestling with the Lord as though he could beat Him. Sort of like a small child wrestling with Hulk Hogan. You know, when you wrestle with little kids, and maybe they hit you and you act like you really got hurt and you fall back—whoa!—and they are thinking they are really tough. That's what it was like. The Lord was humoring Jacob. As He wrestled with him, He would put up some resistance and then let Jacob prevail a little bit, and then press him some more, and then let him prevail a little bit more.

What was this all about? God was waiting for Jacob to run out of strength. He was waiting for him to give up. And finally Jacob is exhausted. He has no energy left. And he goes from cunning to clinging—from resisting to resting. And he is hanging onto the Lord. The Lord says, "Let Me go. I've got to go." And Jacob says, "I am not going to let You go until You bless me." Now, that was a valid request on Jacob's part—asking for this blessing—for in surrender to God's plan he would find what he always wanted.

Here is some interesting commentary on this event from Hosea 12:3–4: "Even in the womb, Jacob struggled with his brother; when he became a man, he even fought with God. Yes, he wrestled with the angel and won. He wept and pleaded for a blessing from him. There at Bethel he met God face to face, and God spoke to him" (NLT). Interesting verbiage: "He wrestled with the angel and won. He wept and pleaded for a blessing." This is the proper kind of wrestling with God, when you are desperately calling out to Him and not giving up because you believe what you ask for is His very will.

IF YOU ARE GOING TO STRUGGLE, LET IT BE IN PRAYER

There is a place for wrestling with God in prayer, in the proper way. Paul mentioned that Epaphras, one of his coworkers in ministry, "is always wrestling in prayer for you," speaking to the Colossian church (Colossians 4:12 NIV). And again in Romans, Paul alludes to this kind of persistence and struggle in prayer when he says, "Dear brothers and sisters, I urge you in the name of our Lord Jesus Christ to join in my struggle by praying to God for me. Do this because of your love for me, given to you by the Holy Spirit" (Romans 15:30 NLT). You see, sometimes prayer can be a struggle. We have wrestling matches where we say, "Lord, I am not going to let You go until You bless me."

There is a place for wrestling with God in prayer.

And we see these wrestling matches in other places in Scripture as well. We see Abraham, for example, praying with persistent intensity for Sodom in Genesis 18, interceding for them. We find Moses spending 40 days and nights fasting and pleading for Israel when God was ready to judge them in Deuteronomy 9. We find Elijah pressed to the ground with his face between his knees, praying seven times for God to send rain in 1 Kings 18. We see this kind of prayer from David, crying out to the Lord in Psalm 39:12, "Hear my prayer, O LORD, and give ear to my cry; do not be silent at my tears."

"Lord, I am not going to let go until You bless me. I am going to keep praying." There are certain things you just don't give up on. You don't give up praying for that unsaved person. I don't care if it seems they have gotten further from God. You keep praying. Keep praying that God will get their attention.

Unless the Lord has directed you otherwise, you keep praying for healing. Keep praying for the will of God to be revealed in your life. **Keep praying; don't give up.** Keep praying for open doors in ministry. Keep praying that God would send a spiritual awakening to your community, to your state, and to your nation. Keep praying; don't give up.

DO YOU REALLY WANT TO CHANGE?

After Jacob's wrestling match, the Lord asked him a provocative question in Genesis 32:27: "What is your name?" Now, why did the Lord ask this of Jacob? Because He didn't know his name? Of course not. God asked it because for Jacob it was an admission— an admission he did not necessarily want to make, because the meaning of his name, *Jacob*, is essentially "heel catcher, supplanter, grabber." In essence, the Lord was saying, "Are you going to continue living up to your name, deceiving others, or will you admit what you are and let me change you?" The Lord could ask the same thing of us in our worrisome lives. "Do you really want to change?"

Some people don't want to change. They don't want to get out of the behavior that they are in. They prefer the ways of sin. Oswald Chambers said, "Sin enough and you will soon be unconscious of sin."

So the Lord effectively says, "Jacob, I have a question for you. Do you want to still be the conniver? Do you want to still be the supplanter? Or do you want to change? Would you like a new name?"

God asks, because He will not force His way into our lives. Jesus says, "Come to Me, all you who labor and are heavy laden, and I will give you rest. Take My yoke upon you and learn from Me" (Matthew 11:28–29). What does it mean when He says, "Take My yoke upon you?" Well, a yoke is a steering device for oxen. So if Jesus had given that statement today, He probably would have said something along the lines of, "Give the steering wheel of your life over to Me."

RELINQUISHING THE CONTROLS

Giving God the steering wheel is easier for some than it is for others. I don't like anyone to drive me anywhere. I like to drive the car. And anyone who has ever driven with me can tell you this because I am the worst backseat driver you have ever met—not just with my wife. I was talking with one of my fellow pastors and he mentioned that when I was the passenger in his car, I kept telling him what to do and I wasn't even aware of it. I said, "There is a good spot. Get in there. Pull in now. *Pull in now.* Get ahead of that guy." I can't help myself.

> The Lord says, "Give Me the steering wheel of your life. Let Me have control."

The Lord says, "Give Me the steering wheel of your life. Let Me have control."

Jacob has been scheming, trying to make it all happen in his own strength, and he has met with nothing but failure after failure after failure. The Lord is saying, "I promised it. I will deliver it. But I like to do My work in My way. Are you up for that? Do you want to change your ways, Jacob?"

Jacob agrees. And a new name is given to him. And that new name is *Israel*. What does Israel mean? Scholars differ as to what it should be translated to say. Some translate it as, "One whom God commands" or "Let God rule." Another translation is, "One who fights victoriously with God." Another translation: "A prince with God." Even another: "God's fighter." But in essence I think we can say it means that there is a complete surrender that took place in Jacob's life, to God and His will. Jacob is no longer the heel catcher and supplanter. Now he is a prince with God, God's fighter.

Now God Himself would be his advocate and Jacob's loss has become Jacob's victory. Through loss comes gain. How can that be? Because up to this point he had been fighting for his will, his plan, his purpose. Losing. Losing. Losing. Reaping what he sows. Time after time. Finally, he is worn out. He has run out of schemes. No more ideas. It is a mess. God says, "Now will you just say 'Uncle'— or better yet 'Father'—and let Me win?"

There has to come a moment where you surrender.

CHANGE COMES THROUGH SURRENDER

And immediately when he submits to the will of God, it all starts coming together so beautifully. "Here is My plan. Here is the way you do it, Jacob. Here is the way to see it take place."

Maybe you have been fighting with God. *I don't want to do it that way. I don't want the Lord to have access to that one area of my life. I don't want to let go of this sin. This is something I really like to do. I don't want to let the Lord give His direction on how I use my finances. I don't want to slow down. I don't want the Lord to tell me I can't. I don't want to stop worrying. I don't want the Lord to tell me to do this thing or go to that place. I want to stay in charge.* Oh, no. There has to come a moment where you surrender. But through your loss gain will come.

> **God's plan for you is better than your plan for yourself.**

And this is exactly what Jesus meant when He said, "If you lose your life for My sake you will find it." We are afraid to lose our life because, to us, it means losing control. But when you give God control of your life, my, how things will change for you.

Are you fighting with God right now? I suggest you surrender. And you will find what you have been looking for all along. Because God's plan for you is better than your plan for yourself. As Corrie ten Boom once said, "Don't wrestle. Just nestle."

FEAR
WORRY
ANXIETY

Proverbs 12:25 tells us, "Anxiety in the heart of man causes depression . . ." The prevalence of anxiety across the country and around the world has reached crisis level, and the problem continues to grow—especially among young people. A recent Pew Research poll[2] indicates that teens see anxiety and depression as the number-one problem among their peers. It ranks above bullying, above drugs and alcohol, above poverty, teen pregnancy, and gangs.

---

2   https://www.pewsocialtrends.org/2019/02/20/most-u-s-teens-see-anxiety-and-depression-as-a-major-problem-among-their-peers/psdt_02-20-19_teens-00-00/

The pressures our young people face are fierce—more intense than the generations that preceded them. Academic demands, social pressure, and stresses at home all combine to place today's youth in a vice of worry.

But the problem is not just limited to young people. I read a statistic that anxiety disorders affect 40 million American adults each year. That's 18.1 percent of the population.[3]

According to a report from the Centers for Disease Control, suicide rates have increased over the nearly two decades leading up to 2016 in 49 out of 50 states in America, with 25 of those states seeing an increase of more than 30 percent.[4]

Those who are only willing to see the problem from a physical, mental, or emotional angle are left baffled by both the cause as well as the solution to this epidemic. And while those are important factors to consider, the spiritual component cannot be neglected. As in all other areas of life, when we try to take God out of the equation, we do so at our peril.

---

3   https://adaa.org/about-adaa/press-room/facts-statistics

4   https://www.cdc.gov/media/releases/2018/p0607-suicide-prevention.html

ANXIETY AND DEPRESSION DESPITE SUCCESS

It wasn't long ago that we were startled by the news of Anthony Bourdain, who took his own life by hanging. It happened right on the heels of a wave of other suicides from famous notables. These included musician/singers Chris Cornell and Chester Bennington, and fashion designer Kate Spade. All of them hanged themselves.

Anthony Bourdain, talented chef and unique storyteller, would travel the world, sample international food, and talk to the locals to create fascinating episodes of *Parts Unknown* a popular and successful TV program. It was a lifestyle that many would look at with envy.

Anthony would ask simple questions about how people cooked, what they ate, and what made them happy. Apparently, he himself did not find the elusive happiness that he pursued worldwide.

Despite his world travels, Anthony was left empty. Like so many other celebrities, businessmen, athletes, and superstars who achieve the success they work toward, perhaps Anthony found that there's nothing at the top of the mountain once you've scaled it.

Have you ever wondered why the rich and famous often have depression, substance abuse issues, or other serious problems? Perhaps it's because they get to do what others only dream of, and they have seen the emptiness that comes with it all. They accomplish a certain level of success and just go on to the next project. The high doesn't last, so they move on to the next thing, and the next, hoping for some sort of satisfaction.

Anthony Bourdain was quoted to have said, "Your body is not a temple. It's an amusement park. Enjoy the ride." Following the pleasures of this life can be enjoyable for a season. But the thrill doesn't last, and so we turn to something else, and then something else—perhaps something illicit, something dangerous, something addictive.

PURSUING PLEASURE

Has there ever been a more pleasure-mad culture than ours today? It seems that we can't be entertained enough. We have continuous media coming our way with constant imagery and sound, all designed to bring us pleasure.

In fact, some people would say, "For me, life means living for pleasure. You know, it's all about having a good time. It's all about the weekend. It's all about the next party. It's all about the next thrill in life."

That philosophy is nothing new. The apostle Paul's contemporary, the emperor Nero, believed that the purpose of life was to live as an unbridled beast in pleasure, passion, and parties. And that is exactly how he lived.

There also was a Greek philosophical group at that time who called themselves the Epicureans. Basically, these were people who lived for pleasure. And we still have people like this today. In fact, the Bible tells us that one of the signs of the last days is that people will be "lovers of pleasure rather than lovers of God" (2 Timothy 3:4). What a waste to live this way, because the Bible says that "she who lives in pleasure is dead while she lives" (1 Timothy 5:6).

I think that Christians are sometimes reluctant to admit that sin isn't always miserable. In fact, the writer of Hebrews said that Moses "refused to be called the son of Pharaoh's daughter, choosing rather to suffer affliction with the people of God than to enjoy the passing pleasures of sin" (11:24–25). Sin can definitely be pleasurable, for a time.

> For a moment of pleasure, you can have a lifetime of regret.

But sin comes with a price—a hefty price. I'm sure it would be very pleasurable to jump out of an airplane and fly through the air without a parachute.

I think it would be the ultimate rush. I think it would be better than any roller coaster or any amusement. But then you are going to hit the ground. So there is fun for a time, but inevitably there is a payday.

There will be pleasure in sin for a season—temporarily. But then the repercussions kick in. The Bible warns that "the wages of sin is death" (Romans 6:23). For a moment of pleasure, you can have a lifetime of regret.

Joy Davidman, the wife of C. S. Lewis, made this insightful statement about the pursuit of pleasure: "Living for his own pleasure is the least pleasurable thing a man can do; if his neighbors don't kill him in disgust, he will die slowly of boredom and loveless-ness." And that is true. It has been said that the only cure for hedonism is to try and practice it.

The pursuit of pleasure is nothing new. As Solomon reminds us a number of times in the Book of Ecclesiastes, when you boil it down, there is nothing new under the sun. Though our technology has changed and we have had certain advance-ments since Solomon wrote those words, the basic cravings of humanity have not changed, nor have the basic things we look to. The philosophy of eat, drink, and be merry has been with us for a long time.

> **When we see God for who He is, we will see the world for what it is.**

When Solomon decided he would pursue everything this world had to offer, he was not considering God in all of it. He was living horizontally—he had adapted a worldview that omitted God. Eventually he came to realize there was nothing to profit from under the sun. It was only when Solomon looked above the sun and looked to God that he found the answers he was seeking. When we see God for who He is, we will see the world for what it is.

ANXIETY AND GUILT

Another reason so many people experience anxiety and depression stems from guilt.

Many people today feel guilty for one simple reason: they *are* guilty. The Bible says we are all guilty before a holy God. And all the psychological counseling in the world cannot relieve a person of that guilt. You can pretend it's not there or find someone else to blame for your problems, but the only real and effective way to remove guilt is to get to the root of the problem, which plainly is sin.

The only real and effective way to remove guilt is to get to the root of the problem, which plainly is sin.

There are a lot of people today who have a guilty conscience. That is what Sir Arthur Conan Doyle, author of the Sherlock Holmes stories, discovered. One day he decided to play a joke on 12 of his friends. He sent them all a message that said, "Flee at once. All is discovered." And within 24 hours, all 12 of his friends had left the country. It was just a joke. Nothing was discovered. But these people felt so guilty about something that they got out as quickly as they could.

Guilt can be good—it can be God's warning system to alert us to a problem. When I am beginning to do something wrong, guilt kicks in. It says, "Stop! Red alert! Don't go any further. This is a bad thing." Guilt is there to remind us we are crossing the line, and we should not go any further.

Do you have a guilty conscience? Maybe God is telling you something. Maybe you should pay attention to your conscience.

SOME THOUGHTS ON DEPRESSION

There is such thing as clinical depression, and it can have many factors. I'm not a medical doctor and I don't want to be one of these trite or flippant know-it-alls who just throws out simple answers to a complicated issue: "Have more faith," or "Trust God more" or "It's all in your head, so just think happy thoughts." That type of thinking doesn't help anyone.

So, if you are suffering from clinical depression, and you're reading this book looking for a cure, I don't know that you are going to find it. There may be physical, mental, or chemical issues in your body that I simply can't speak to. But the spiritual principles remain true for everyone, even for you.

So let me speak to those who are experiencing depression in the sense that they are "down in the dumps." You might be in the doldrums even though you are in good health, you had a meal today, and you have clothes on your back and a roof over your head. Maybe you are down because you know someone else has it a little better—or maybe a whole lot better—than you do. If so, then I have a 10-step solution for your depression.

Step Number 1: Do something for someone else who has greater needs than you.

Step Number 2: Repeat step Number 1 nine more times.

Not only has God told us it is happier to give than to receive, but scientific research shows the same. It is well documented that volunteering elevates mood in most people. This phenomenon has been dubbed "the helper's high." It has been assessed biologically in brain-imaging studies. It has also been looked at in research on endorphins.

I have never experienced the "runner's high," but I do know about the "giver's high." If someone asks you what you are doing on the weekend, you can say, "Getting high!" Whoa, what? "Yes, at church, giving to the Lord and serving others!" Proverbs 11:25 says that those who refresh others are themselves refreshed.

When we take our eyes off ourselves, it puts things into perspective. As a pastor, I visit people in hospitals. I can have the sniffles and be thinking, "Poor me," and then go and visit someone who is in critical condition. I leave just thanking God that I can walk out of the hospital.

The Bible tells us to "do nothing out of selfish ambition or vain conceit. Rather, in humility value others above yourselves" (Philippians 2:3 NIV). In other words, never let selfishness or conceit become your motive in life.

Selfishness is at the root of almost all sins. Most of the quarrels and conflicts we have in life occur because self is either being threatened, challenged, or ignored. It is all about us. As James 4:1 asks,

"What is causing the quarrels and fights among you? Don't they come from the evil desires at war within you?" (NLT). How true is that? We all want our own way. And that is prewired in us from the earliest days. The Bible says, "For everyone has sinned; we all fall short of God's glorious standard" (Romans 3:23 NLT). There is no getting around it: We are all naturally selfish.

Selfishness ruins so many things in life. Why did Adam and Eve eat the forbidden fruit? Because Satan told them, "You will be like God, knowing good and evil" (Genesis 3:5 NIV). They were selfish.

Think of all of the immorality in our culture today. Why do people have sex before marriage? They are selfish. They don't want to wait to commit themselves to each other. They want the fringe benefits of marriage without the commitment that goes along with it. And why do people commit adultery after they have been married? Selfishness. They don't care about their mate; they want to have a little fun.

Do you know someone that has a need right now? Someone you can reach out to? Someone who is hurting? If you wait to feel love for people, you will never do anything. If you wait until you feel like putting that relationship back together, it will never get put back together. Will you do it by faith? Will you do it in obedience? If you will, then you can live a joyful life. But if you run around living for self-fulfillment, then you will be miserable. If you will remember your purpose on earth is to glorify God and to love others, then you will find the personal fulfillment you always wanted. And you will find happiness as well.

AVICII

Did you happen to read about the young Swedish DJ superstar Avicii? This young man, (whose actual name is Tim Bergling) was at the top of his game, making millions of dollars. He had what most young people dream of today: fame and money.

He appeared in jam-packed arenas. He was in constant demand, but that fame took its toll on Avicii's life, and at the age of 28 he committed suicide. And the question is asked, "Why? Why would you do this? Why would you end your life at such a young age?" His family gave the answer when they said, "He really struggled with thoughts about meaning, life, and happiness. He could not go on any longer. He wanted to find peace."

I wish I could've sat down with this young man and said, "Friend, I've got the answers, and you're not going to find them out there in this world's culture.

It's only found in a relationship with God through Jesus Christ."

Avicii is just one of many people that have found this out the hard way.

ELVIS

I saw a documentary the other day on the life of Elvis Presley. Elvis was an amazing person. He was raised in abject poverty. He loved to sing in the church. He loved to sing gospel music. He had an incredible voice and, of course, he became globally famous and had what many people dream of.

But he didn't have happiness. He once said that his life, to him, was miserable: "I feel that I'm sick and tired of my life. I need a long rest." He ended up dying of a prescription drug overdose. And in this documentary that his widow was a part of, she said that she thinks Elvis actually committed suicide.

After Elvis, we saw many others suffer the same fate. Rock icons from the '60s Janis Joplin, Jim Morrison, and Jimi Hendrix all died of drug overdoses at the age of 27.

Fast-forward to more recent times. Michael Jackson, Prince, and others join the list. Tom Petty, who ironically was one of the narrators in the documentary film about Elvis, died not long after because of a prescription drug overdose.

All these people, they had it all, and yet they turned to drugs and some of them ended their lives intentionally. When are people going to learn that the answers are not in the things the world has to offer?

This desire for happiness—it's in us. It's deeply within us. We're hardwired to be happy. So where do we find this happiness? If you look for it in this world, you will end up disappointed because circumstances continually change. If things are going reasonably well, we're happy—for a time. If things are not going so well, then we're unhappy. Someone put it this way: There are two sources of unhappiness in life. One is not getting what you want, and the other is getting it. You see, if you don't get it, you'll say, "Well, if I just had this then I would be happy." But when you get everything, when you have all of your dreams fulfilled, when you reach all those goals and maybe even surpass them, and you find how empty it is then you realize happiness is not in these things at all.

Justin Bieber posted this on Instagram: "Hey world, that glamorous lifestyle portrayed by famous people on Instagram, don't be fooled thinking their life is better than yours. I can promise you it's not."

And I would argue in many cases, those people that you may follow on social media, those people you admire and look up to, may have a far more miserable life than you have.

Is happiness found in having lots of money? Money can buy some things, but not the most important things. Money can buy you a bed, but it can't buy you a good night's sleep. Money can buy you books but not brains. It can buy you a house but not a home. It can buy you medicine but not health. It can buy you amusement but not happiness.

TRUE HAPPINESS

So how do you find happiness? Surveys by Gallup, the National Opinion Research Center, and the Pew Organization conclude that spiritually committed people are twice as likely to report being "very happy" than the least religiously committed people.

So, happy people are spiritual people. But let me take it further: truly happy people are godly people. The Bible says, "Happy are the people whose God is the Lord!" (Psalm 144:15).

According to the Bible, if we seek to know God and discover His plan for our life, we will as a result, find the happiness that has eluded us for so long—not from seeking it but from seeking Him! As Matthew 6:33 says, "Seek first the kingdom of God and His righteousness, and all these things shall be added to you."

C. S. Lewis said, "God designed the human machine to run on Himself. He Himself is the fuel our spirits were designed to burn, or the food our spirits were designed to feed on. There is no other. That is why it is just no good asking God to make us happy in our own way without bothering about [faith]. God cannot give us a happiness and peace apart from Himself, because it is not there. There is no such thing."

According to the Scriptures, happiness is never something that should be sought directly. It is always something that results from seeking something else.

If we seek holiness, we'll find happiness.

And what is holiness? The word holiness has gotten a bad rap. If you hear that a person is "holier than thou," it is not a good thing. But true holiness is not a fake, condescending, or mystical thing. Holiness can be understood better if we spell it another way: whollyness.

It was said of Caleb, "He wholly followed the Lord God" (Joshua 14:14). When you wholly follow God, you will be a holy person—and a happy one too!

We find what we are looking for in life by seeking God, not seeking "it." Henry Ward Beecher once said, "The strength of a man consists in finding out the way in which God is going, and going in that way too."

So, if you want to be happy, be holy. In other words, live a life that's wholly committed to Him.

GOD WANTS YOU TO BE HAPPY

Yes, happiness is found in God. And here's something you need to know: God wants you to be happy.

Isn't that good news? You might have a hard time believing that based on a perception of God that you've grown up with or your past experiences. But it's true. He actually does want us to be happy. I know this because He tells us so in Scripture. He tells us over and over again that this happiness is something that He wants us to experience in a relationship with us.

In the Bible, the word *blessed* is another translation for the word *happy*. They're interchangeable words. So when we read the word *blessed*, as we do in the Beatitudes, you can just take that word out and put in the word *happy*. Really, the theme of the Beatitudes, which is the point of entry into the Sermon on the Mount, is happiness—how you can be happy.

You're going to find a biblical worldview by studying Scripture, and in particular by zeroing in on the Sermon on the Mount. Do you want to know how Jesus thinks? Do you want to know how His heart beats? Do you want to know what He feels about living and about life in general? Study the Sermon on the Mount. It is the manifesto of the King of kings and the Lord of lords.

Let's quickly look at Matthew 5, where we find the Beatitudes. These are the opening words of the Sermon on the Mount. Matthew 5:2 says that Jesus "opened His mouth and taught them." Taught who? His disciples. These words are for followers of Jesus Christ. He said,

> Blessed are the poor in spirit,
>> For theirs is the kingdom of heaven.
> Blessed are those who mourn,
>> For they shall be comforted.
> Blessed are the meek,
>> For they shall inherit the earth.
> Blessed are those who hunger and thirst for
>> righteousness,
>> For they shall be filled.

Blessed are the merciful,
> For they shall obtain mercy.
Blessed are the pure in heart,
> For they shall see God.
Blessed are the peacemakers,
> For they shall be called sons of God.
Blessed are those who are persecuted for righteousness' sake,
> For theirs is the kingdom of heaven.

Blessed are you when they revile and persecute you, and say all kinds of evil against you falsely for My sake. Rejoice and be exceedingly glad, for great is your reward in heaven, for so they persecuted the prophets who were before you.

> *Matthew 5:3–12*

Blessed, or again, *happy* are these people. How different the Beatitudes are from modern culture! If the Beatitudes were rewritten for culture today, they would go along these lines:

Blessed are the beautiful,
> for they shall be admired.
Blessed are the wealthy,
> for they will have it all.

Blessed are the popular,
>for they will be loved.
Blessed are the famous,
>for they shall be followed.

But that's not what Jesus says. In fact, He says quite the opposite. There is so much rich content in the Sermon on the Mount that I could write volumes on it. But let me summarize Jesus' main points in the Beatitudes so that we can understand the basics of how to find happiness.

1. **Happy are the nobodies.** "Blessed are the poor in spirit." To be poor in spirit is not speaking of how much money you have or don't have in your bank account. It means to recognize your real spiritual state before God. You are spiritually destitute, bankrupt. You are a sinner. You are lost, hopeless, and helpless— effectively a nobody.

2. **Happy people are unhappy people.** "Blessed are those who mourn, for they shall be comforted," or blessed are the unhappy for they will be happy. When I see my condition before God and I am sorry for it, it causes me to grieve and be sorrowful for my condition.

3. **Happy are the humble.** "Blessed are the meek." When I see myself as I really am and then mourn over my condition, I will have a change in attitude. Instead of arrogance there is a new humility that comes from seeing things as they are. I recognize that if it weren't for the grace of God I would be nowhere.

4. **Happy are the spiritually hungry.** "Blessed are those who hunger and thirst for righteousness, for they shall be filled." A happy person desires a righteous life. With the new humility there is a thirst for godliness, and as you take in more of the things of God, you find satisfaction.

5. **Happy people are merciful people.** "Blessed are the merciful, for they shall obtain mercy." If I see myself as a sinner, and I weep over my sin, it produces in me a humility and a hunger and a thirst to know Christ and become more like Him. That is going to make me a person who is merciful to others.

6. **A happy person is a holy person.** "Blessed are the pure in heart, for they shall see God." To be pure of heart is to have a focus centered

on your relationship with God and to pursue purity in all that you do.

7. **A happy person will be a peacemaker.** "Blessed are the peacemakers." It is not about world peace. It is about personal peace with God. Before we were Christians, we were at war with God. The Bible says that we experience peace after we are justified through Jesus Christ. Then we do everything we can to bring others into a relationship with the Lord so they can be at peace with Him too.

8. **A happy person will be persecuted.** "Blessed are those who are persecuted for righteousness' sake, for theirs is the kingdom of heaven." If you live a godly life, you will be persecuted. But God will be with you in your persecution and will give you the peace, joy, and strength you need to endure it.

So again, we find that as we seek holiness, we will find happiness as a byproduct.

GOD'S ANSWER FOR FEAR WORRY ANXIETY

Often, people who are hostile to God say that Christians use religion as a crutch. I say it isn't a crutch; it is an entire hospital!

Everyone leans on something—even the hostile cynic. That something we lean on could be a friend, a husband or wife, a career, or a bank balance. You may be relying on yourself or even on religion, but these are flimsy props that won't hold up for long, if at all.

When we lean on Jesus, we're leaning on the only One who can sustain us. We all need help. We're all essentially weak. We all need someone to comfort us and reassure us, and most importantly, forgive us of our sins.

FIRST THINGS FIRST

If you are in a crisis right now, if you are facing fear, worry, anxiety, or depression at this moment, but you are not a follower of Christ, this is the time to admit that you need Jesus.

When the storms hit your life and send you reeling, when your friends let you down, when your money is spent, and you are left all alone, it is time to call on God. He is anxiously awaiting your cry.

As a young boy growing up in Southern California, I liked to surf. One day, a big set of towering overhead waves came rolling in while I was paddling out. When that happens, you're supposed to head toward the waves and go underneath them, which goes against every natural inclination you have. Your instinct is to turn away from the waves and toward the shore. On this afternoon, I dove under one wave after another and got further and further from shore. A rip tide then started to pull me out even further, and I suddenly knew I was in trouble. I was exhausted from trying to penetrate those mountains of water, and I could barely see my friends back on the beach. All I had to do to be out of this situation was to yell, "Help!" But I was too proud. I thought, "I'd rather die than have to be rescued by a lifeguard." I almost did!

How foolish we are not to call for help when we need it. Hand your burdens and problems over to the

Lord. He will carry them for you. Jesus said, "Come to Me, all you who labor and are heavy laden, and I will give you rest" (Matthew 11:28).

God invites you to bring your problems and heartaches and troubles, all your fears and worries, to Him. As the apostle Peter said, "[Cast] all your care upon Him, for He cares for you" (1 Peter 5:7). Jesus has already paid the price for you at the cross of Calvary, and He wants to help you through this situation too. He will answer the minute you call upon Him.

A lumberjack once stood by a river as felled trees floated downstream. He watched carefully as each tree rushed past. He would often hook a limb and pull it to shore only to toss the tree back into the current. Surprisingly, he only seemed interested in the most worn pieces and allowed the fresh trunks and branches to float away.

When he was asked the reason for his choices, he replied, "You only see the outside bark. But I know that those trees you think are healthy come from the side of the mountain that is protected from the winds and the rains. These other logs here, they come from high on the mountain where they have withstood incredible storms. That is where we get the tough lumber. And I save it for my choicest work." You too have been chosen by God for His purposes. Let your contentment come from the One who has given His life for you.

After Jesus had calmed the sea, His disciples exclaimed, "Who can this be, that even the wind and the sea obey Him!" (Mark 4:41). This question is answered only in the truth that He was both God and man. He was more than a great teacher or a leader. He was God who walked among us as a human, and He was with them through the storm.

When Christ died on the cross, it was not just a great man who died; it was the God-man. When He took the sin of the world upon Himself, He acted not as a mere prophet or a spiritual leader; He acted as God Himself. Even the man next to Jesus on the cross turned and called on Him for salvation. In those last moments of his life, Jesus did not turn him away. Jesus forgave the thief and assured him of everlasting life.

Jesus is asking you to bring your problems, your fears, and your worries to Him. Call on the name of the Lord. Replace your fear and worry with trust and faith. The same Jesus who calmed the seas for those troubled disciples gripped by fear and worry is standing at the door of your heart right now. He says, "Behold, I stand at the door and knock. If anyone hears My voice and opens the door, I will come in" (Revelation 3:20).

If you would like to trust Jesus Christ as Lord and Savior, simply ask Him to forgive you of your sins.

You can do this through prayer, which is just talking to God. Ask Him to take control of your life and show you how to live a life of true fulfillment based on His grace. From this day forward, you will be glad you did. The seas may not always be calm, but you can know that He is directing the winds that blow your way and will see you through all your storms.

If you need a place to start, consider these words:

> Lord Jesus, I know that I am a sinner, and I am sorry for my sin. I thank You for dying on the cross for me. I turn from my sin, and I turn to You by faith right now. Forgive me for all of the wrong things I have done. Fill me with the power of Your Holy Spirit. I want to be Your disciple. Help me to love You and hate sin from this time forward. Thank You for Your offer of forgiveness. I gladly accept it now. In Your name I pray. Amen.

If you've prayed that prayer, I would love to hear from you. I would also like to send you some helpful materials, at no cost, to encourage you in your spiritual growth. Please write to me or visit KnowGod.org.

For those who are reading this book that are already Christians, or if you've just prayed that prayer and have begun to trust the Lord, I want you to consider a powerful tool to combat fear, worry, and anxiety: worship.

THE ROLE OF WORSHIP

The Bible gives us some amazing examples of people who overcame fear, worry, and anxiety. They countered these things by trusting the Lord and worshipping Him.

Take Paul and Silas for instance. Their story is found in Acts 16:16–40. If anyone had reason to be afraid, worried, or anxious, it is these two men in a dark, dank prison cell in Philippi. And yet they chose to worship. Let's examine the account of these two men. First, a little background on Philippi to give you context.

Philippi was a Roman colony. The Romans had effectively conquered a good deal of the world, including Greece, and they would build little Roman colonies in each place. They would encourage Roman citizens to move to these other places so they would have loyal subjects there. They wanted pro-Roman cities in strategic areas—a "Rome away from Rome," if you will. And people could visit these cities and they would find a lot of things they had in Rome, on a smaller scale. For example, they might have their own little amphitheater—it wouldn't be anything like the enormous Coliseum, but it would be in the same vein. A lot of the luxuries of Rome but on a smaller scale. That is what Philippi was. It was in an area of Greece but was now a Roman city. And in this city, there was a lot of anti-Semitism. So this is what Paul was seeing in Philippi, and as a Jew, he was going to have to face this bigotry toward the Jewish people.

Paul comes into town and he goes looking for the synagogue, but there was no synagogue. It would seem there were not enough Jews in this city to form a synagogue. You needed ten Jewish men to form a synagogue, and because apparently there weren't that many Jewish men there, Paul went down to the river where some Jewish women were meeting. Among them was a woman named Lydia. Lydia was a very affluent woman. The Bible tells us she was a "seller of purple." Now, that doesn't mean anything to us today, but it means she sold expensive clothing that was dyed purple—a color of luxury.

The Bible says that as she listened to Paul, the Lord opened her heart, and she accepted what Paul was saying. She then was baptized along with other members of her household. And after her conversion,

Paul and Silas were followed around town by a demon-possessed girl. And strangely she yelled out, "These men are servants of the Most High God, and they have come to tell you how to be saved." What she was saying was true, but she was possessed by demons and she shrieked it. Paul was thinking, "Is she ever going to stop?" And this went on for days. Finally Paul couldn't take it anymore and he cast the demon out of her. And along with that went her ability to make money because she worked for her masters as a fortune-teller. She was a slave girl, and they were making a lot of money from this witchy woman. So now the masters were angry with Paul and Silas, and they dragged them down to the town square.

"The whole city is in an uproar because of these Jews!" they shouted to the city officials. "They are teaching customs that are illegal for us Romans to practice" (Acts 16:20–22 NLT). A mob quickly formed against Paul and Silas, and the city officials ordered them stripped and beaten with wooden rods.

So the accusers of Paul and Silas cleverly exploited the rampant anti-Semitism. Notice that they refer to Paul and Silas as "these Jews." And then they appeal to Roman pride. "It is not according to Roman customs!" They brought Paul and Silas up on false charges, and they beat them with wooden rods.

They were severely beaten, and then they were thrown into prison. The jailer was ordered to make sure they didn't escape. So the jailer put them into the inner dungeon and clamped their feet in the stocks.

WORSHIP INSTEAD OF WORRY

What a fearful position to be in. If ever there was a time to feel anxious or worried, this might be it. But the Bible says that at midnight Paul and Silas were praying and singing hymns to God, and the other prisoners were listening.

Suddenly, there was a massive earthquake, and the prison was shaken to its foundations. All the doors immediately flew open, and the chains of every prisoner fell off! The jailer woke up to see the prison doors wide open. He assumed the prisoners had escaped, so he drew his sword to kill himself. But Paul shouted to him, "Stop! Don't kill yourself! We are all here!"

The jailer called for lights and ran to the dungeon and fell down trembling before Paul and Silas. Then he brought them out and asked, "Sirs, what must I do to be saved?"

They replied, "Believe in the Lord Jesus and you will be saved, along with everyone in your household" (Acts 16:31 NLT). And they shared the Word of the Lord with him and with all who lived in his household. Even at that hour of the night, the jailer cared for them and washed their wounds. Then he and everyone in his household were immediately baptized. He brought them into his house and set a meal before them, and he and his entire household rejoiced because they all believed in God.

Wow. What a story. Paul starts out in prison and he ends up leading the jailer to the Lord. But what set the scene for this dramatic chain of events is found in Acts 16:24: they are clamped in stocks. Just imagine how horrific this is. I mean, when we talk about dungeons of the first century, we are talking about the worst conditions imaginable. There is no ventilation. There is no sanitation. It is just a cave. It is a pit of death and misery. And then, if that weren't bad enough, they are put into these stocks where their legs are spread apart causing excruciating pain. Would you be feeling a bit of fear, worry, or anxiety in their situation?

There they are in agony, facing an unknown outcome, and what do they do? They offered a sacrifice of praise. At midnight, Paul and Silas began to sing praises to God.

SONGS IN THE NIGHT

You know, when you are in pain, the midnight hour is not the easiest time for a worship service. But God can give songs in the night. Psalm 42:8 says, "Each day the Lord pours his unfailing love upon me, and through each night I sing his songs, praying to God who gives me life" (NLT).

Have you ever woken up in the middle of the night and had a Christian song, a worship chorus, going through your mind? Isn't that cool? Do you know what that says to me? It says that you are laying up the things of God in your heart. Instead of waking up to the lyrics of "Wild Thing" in your head, you wake up and you have a Christian song, or maybe a Scripture, just playing through your mind. That is a song in the night that the Lord has given to you.

So Paul and Silas were singing songs from prison and Acts 16:25 tells us that the other prisoners were listening to them. Now the word that is used here for *listen* is significant. It means to listen very carefully. Another way to translate it is, they listened with pleasure. There are some things that are not a pleasure to listen to, like fingernails on a chalkboard. But this was pleasurable. It is like when your favorite song comes on the radio and you go to turn it up. "Oh, I love this song. This is a great song!" Their fellow prisoners were listening with pleasure.

Why? Well, I doubt they had ever heard anyone sing in that dungeon before. Now, I don't know if Paul and Silas were harmonizing, but I think just the fact that they were singing to the Lord was a powerful testimony. It was a platform for evangelism. You can talk about trusting God in adversity but when someone sees it in action in your life, there is an undeniable authenticity. It is a powerful witness. You can tell your nonbelieving friends, "I am a Christian and God is in control of my life" but it might just be words to them until something horrific happens to you and they see you are still praising God. That carries a lot of weight. That makes your words more powerful. And the next time you talk to them, they are going to listen more carefully.

That is why I believe worship can be a powerful tool for a nonbeliever to witness. I think it is a good thing when people come to church and see believers worshipping the Lord. That is a powerful testimony. They are not just checking out what is happening on the platform; they are also checking out what is happening around them. And if they see that people are engaged and worshipping God, they are thinking, "Wow. These people are into this." On the other hand, if people are distracted or talking to their friends or whatever, then that says to them, "This must not be all that important."

So this was a powerful testimony. And some-thing supernatural happens when God's people come together and engage in corporate worship. It is great to worship by yourself, but when two or more are gathered together in His name, He is there in the midst of them (see Matthew 18:20). That doesn't mean that God is not with us everywhere

> When we worship on earth, we are in tune with what is happening in Heaven.

we go, because the fact of the matter is that God is omnipresent, which means present everywhere. Yet it is an undeniable fact that when God's people get together and pray and worship together, the Lord blesses it in a wonderful way. And that is why church is important.

When we worship on earth, we are in tune with what is happening in Heaven, because in Heaven worship is constantly in motion. Revelation 5:12 says, "They sang in a mighty chorus: 'Worthy is the Lamb who was slaughtered—to receive power and riches and wisdom and strength and honor and glory and blessing'" (NLT). So in Heaven, praises are being offered. When we are praising the Lord on earth, we are joining the chorus of Heaven. And God is looking for people to worship Him in spirit and in truth (see John 4:23).

WORSHIP BRINGS PERSPECTIVE

When we come to church and worship, it helps us get things into perspective. Asaph asked the age-old question, "Why do the wicked prosper?" And then it's like the answer dawned on him in Psalm 73:16–17: "When I tried to figure it out, all I got was a splitting headache . . . until I entered the sanctuary of God. Then I saw the whole picture" (MSG).

Sometimes we don't understand why things are the way that they are. But when we come and worship and we hear the Word of God, even if it doesn't apply specifically to our situation, it helps us get perspective.

When our son Christopher died on a Thursday, we were in church the following Sunday. And people said, "Oh Greg, your faith is so strong." No, actually my faith was weak. I needed help. I needed God's people. I needed to worship God. I needed to hear a Bible study. I needed perspective. And I will tell you, the moment I walked in and was surrounded by God's people and I knew they were praying for me, it helped me. It is not like all my questions were answered and it was all good. No. It was still as painful as ever. But it helped me get perspective. When you worship the Lord, you see God for who He is and you see your problems for what they are. Sometimes we have big problems because we have a small God. But if we have a big God we will see, comparatively speaking, we have small problems. That is why church is important. That is why hearing the Word of God preached to you is important.

So Paul and Silas had perspective and they praised God in a stinking dungeon.

Three or four years later Paul is in prison again. And this time there hasn't been an earthquake, but he is still singing. In fact he writes about it in Philippians. Consider these words of Paul that were written in a prison cell:

> Always be full of joy in the Lord. I say it again—rejoice! Let everyone see that you are considerate in all you do. Remember, the Lord is coming soon.
>
> Don't worry about anything; instead, pray about everything. Tell God what you need, and thank him for all he has done. Then you will experience God's peace, which exceeds anything we can understand. His peace will guard your hearts and minds as you live in Christ Jesus.
>
> *Philippians 4:4–7 NLT*

Now, that is interesting, because when He says, "Always be full of joy in the Lord. I say it again—rejoice!" it is a command. You are commanded by God to rejoice, whether you feel like it or not. Paul was not living in the lap of luxury when he wrote these words; he was actually in a prison cell. If anyone had reason to be depressed, it'd be Paul. But he chose to rejoice, and you and I should too. Rejoice in the Lord always!

Rejoice in the Lord always!

And that is what Paul and Silas were doing with their songs in the night. You know, only a person with a relationship with God can truly do this. Our joy and contentment in life do not come from what we have, but who we know.

Now, whatever you get in life, you are going to get tired of it in time, right? What is better than a new car? Don't you love the new car smell? You look for excuses to go on a drive so you can get in your new car. And you make a vow: "I am never going to eat in this car." Then a month goes by and you are late for work and you have to eat. You get a burrito, and you lose it somewhere in the car. You don't know where it went. And then you get your first dent. Someone opens a door and bumps it. And then the paint chips a little bit. And then, you know what? What was once new and exciting isn't so exciting anymore.

Take that metaphor and apply it to everything in life, and it remains true. I don't care how big, how cool, or how fast it is—everything loses its appeal after a period of time. So if you think happiness comes from what you have, you will find that you are always going to want something else to take its place.

But the Bible teaches that happiness—true happiness—comes not from what we have, but from God. Habakkuk 3:17–18 says,

> Even though the fig trees have no blossoms, and there are no grapes on the vines; even though the olive crop fails, and the fields lie empty and barren; even though the flocks die in the fields, and the cattle barns are empty, yet I will rejoice in the Lord! I will be joyful in the God of my salvation! (NLT)

Let me update that for modern times: Even when business is slow and there are no prospects in the immediate future, even when my investments have evaporated and the car won't start, when depression and anxiousness are biting at my heels, I will rejoice in the Lord.

The words of a crazy man? No. The words of a man who recognizes that contentment does not come from what you have. It comes from who you know. And that is how Paul and Silas were able to rejoice in these circumstances.

So here are Paul and Silas. At midnight they sing praises to God. I want you to notice that we don't read about them praying for deliverance. They didn't say, "Lord, send an earthquake," or "Lord, remember how You busted Peter out of jail with the angel? How about doing that for us right now?" We don't read that they prayed anything of the kind. They just sang praises to God. And yes, the earthquake came, but that is not the focus of the story. The focus of the story is that the child of God can rejoice in the most trying of circumstances. That is the message. Because you know what? Sometimes the earthquake doesn't happen. Deliverance from circumstances doesn't always come. Sometimes He delivers us *from* our circumstances like He did for Daniel in the lion's den. And sometimes He delivers us in our circumstances like He did for Shadrach, Meshach, and Abednego.

Contentment does not come from what you have. It comes from who you know.

GOD IS WITH YOU

Shadrach, Meshach, and Abednego were thrown into a fiery furnace that was heated seven times hotter than normal because of their unwillingness to bow before the golden image of the king. We read that while they were walking through the furnace, walking with them was one who was like the Son of God, which many of us believe was Christ Himself.

So sometimes you will say, "Lord, help me," and He will deliver you and heal you. He will provide for you. He will fix your problem. And other times He says, "I am going to be with you through it, so trust Me."

We need to keep that in mind. Ultimately, Paul wasn't delivered from that prison in Rome. In fact, he was beheaded. But on this occasion in Philippi, he was delivered. An earthquake came. Paul and Silas were singing, and you could say that they really "brought the house down," right?

An earthquake comes and shakes things up so that the walls of the prison literally collapse. And this Roman soldier is ready to kill himself. Now understand, this is a hard man. After he whipped Paul and Silas, he didn't even wash their wounds. But he noticed they were different. He had heard their songs in the night too. And he might have thought, "What if it is possible to know a God like this?" I think he was already deeply moved by their willingness to worship God.

Why would he think to kill himself when the walls came down? Because back in those days if you were a Roman guard in charge of someone and your prisoner got away, you would be put to death along with your family. So he thought, "I will just have an honorable death and kill myself right now. I am ready to do it." Paul says, "Don't hurt yourself. We are all here. We haven't left."

What does the guy say next? "Sirs, what must I do to be saved?" (Acts 16:30). I love the fact that he called them *sirs*. Very formal. I'm sure he wasn't calling them sirs before this happened. Paul answers, "Believe on the Lord Jesus Christ, and you will be saved" (verse 31). And the man believes. Verse 33 tells us, "Even at that hour of the night, the jailer cared for them and washed their wounds. Then he and everyone in his household were immediately baptized" (NLT).

Like Zacchaeus, the tax collector in Luke 19:8 who made restoration because he stole from people, there was clear evidence of a change of heart demonstrated by this man's actions. When there is no change in actions, it is doubtful there has been a change of heart. If your heart is really changed, your actions will change. And if your actions haven't changed, it is doubtful your heart has really changed.

Paul and Silas could easily have chosen not to worship. They could have thought, "My circumstances stink. I don't feel like worshipping." They could have spent their time grumbling and complaining. They could have been angry or depressed or indignant or fearful. But they chose instead to turn their hearts to the Lord in worship and surrender. And look what happened as a result. Not only were they happier, not only did it bless the Lord to receive their worship, but an entire household came to know the Lord because of their witness of worship.

I pray that all of us who read this book will find a song in the night when things are scary or uncertain or difficult or frustrating. I pray that we would have hearts of worship in every experience, in every circumstance, in every phase of life—from the beginning to the middle, right to the end, and then into eternity.

SOME PRACTICAL
QUESTIONS TO CONSIDER

We have looked at fear, worry, and anxiety from a spiritual perspective because I truly believe at its core, it is a spiritual issue. But that doesn't mean there aren't some physical and mental factors that contribute to these things.

Consider these questions:

- Am I getting enough sleep?
- Am I nourishing my body with the things I eat, or am I filling it with junk?
- Am I hydrated?
- Am I getting exercise on a regular basis?

- When's the last time I took a vacation?
- What images am I filling my mind with?
- How much time am I spending on social media and mindless entertainment?
- Do I interact with others or do I isolate myself?
- Do I have a support network of caring individuals around me?

I think the basic idea behind these questions is the principle that what we put into our minds and bodies has a direct correlation with the things we think and feel.

CONCLUSION

I think the best way to recap the principles we've explored in this book is to go straight to the Scriptures to summarize what we've discussed.

What is God's answer to fear? God's presence expels fear.

> Fear not, for I am with you;
> Be not dismayed, for I am your God.
> I will strengthen you,
> Yes, I will help you,
> I will uphold you with My righteous right hand.
> *Isaiah 41:10*

———

And the Lord, He is the One who goes before you. He will be with you, He will not leave you nor forsake you; do not fear nor be dismayed.

Deuteronomy 31:8

———

Fear not, for I have redeemed you;
    I have called you by your name;
    You are Mine.
When you pass through the waters,
    I will be with you;
And through the rivers,
    they shall not overflow you.
When you walk through the fire,
    you shall not be burned,
    Nor shall the flame scorch you.
For I am the Lord your God,
    The Holy One of Israel, your Savior.

Isaiah 43:1–3

What is God's answer to worry? Turn your worries into prayers!

> Don't worry about anything; instead, pray about everything. Tell God what you need, and thank him for all he has done. Then you will experience God's peace, which exceeds anything we can understand. His peace will guard your hearts and minds as you live in Christ Jesus.
>
> *Philippians 4:6–7 NLT*

> Give all your worries and cares to God, for he cares about you.
>
> *1 Peter 5:7*

> Therefore I say to you, do not worry about your life, what you will eat or what you will drink; nor about your body, what you will put on. Is not life more than food and the body more than clothing? Look at the birds of the air, for they neither sow nor reap nor gather into barns; yet your heavenly Father feeds

them. Are you not of more value than they? Which of you by worrying can add one cubit to his stature?

So why do you worry about clothing? Consider the lilies of the field, how they grow: they neither toil nor spin; and yet I say to you that even Solomon in all his glory was not arrayed like one of these. Now if God so clothes the grass of the field, which today is, and tomorrow is thrown into the oven, will He not much more clothe you, O you of little faith?

Therefore do not worry, saying, "What shall we eat?" or "What shall we drink?" or "What shall we wear?" For after all these things the Gentiles seek. For your heavenly Father knows that you need all these things. But seek first the kingdom of God and His righteousness, and all these things shall be added to you. Therefore do not worry about tomorrow, for tomorrow will worry about its own things. Sufficient for the day is its own trouble.

Matthew 6:25–34

What is God's answer to anxiety? Abide in the Lord, remain close to Him, and draw comfort from His nearness.

But you, O Lord, are a shield around me;
    you are my glory,
      the one who holds my head high.

Psalm 3:3 NLT

———

Blessed is the one who trusts in the Lord,
    whose confidence is in him.
They will be like a tree planted by the water
    that sends out its roots by the stream.
It does not fear when heat comes;
    its leaves are always green.
It has no worries in a year of drought
    and never fails to bear fruit.

Jeremiah 17:7–8 NIV

———

In the multitude of my anxieties within me,
Your comforts delight my soul.

Psalm 94:19

———

The Lord is my shepherd, I lack nothing.
    He makes me lie down in green pastures,
he leads me beside quiet waters,
    he refreshes my soul.
He guides me along the right paths
    for his name's sake.
Even though I walk
    through the darkest valley,
I will fear no evil,
    for you are with me;
your rod and your staff,
    they comfort me.

You prepare a table before me
    in the presence of my enemies.
You anoint my head with oil;
    my cup overflows.
Surely your goodness and love will follow me
    all the days of my life,
and I will dwell in the house of the Lord
    forever.

Psalm 23 NIV